Nashville, Tennessee, by Thomas Nelson, Inc., Publishers, and distributed in Canada by nications, Ltd., Richmond, British Columbia.

ngapore

Library of Congress Cataloging-in-Publication Data

n Rayburn.
ok of prayer / Helen Caswell.
cm.
352-8034-0
—Juvenile literature. 2. Children—Prayer-books and devotions—English. [1. Prayers.
ks and devotions.] I. Title.
1995

)   94-24377
                                                                   CIP
                                                                    AC

3 4 5 6 — 00 99 98 97 96

A Little B
of Praye

Published i
Word Comm

Printed in S

Caswell, He.
    A little b
        p.
    ISBN 0-7
    1. Prayer
2. Prayer bo
BV265.C27
242'.62—dc2

A Little Book of Prayer

Helen Caswell

OLIVER
NELSON

THOMAS NELSON PUBLISHERS
Nashville • Atlanta • London • Vancouver

Praying's easy.
Every morning,
  first of all, I say,
  "Good morning, God!"
  and then
  I talk to Him all day.
  He's never
    very far away.

At the table
I say grace for food,
and ask God's blessing
on my mouth,

~ that only
wholesome food
goes in,
and only
wholesome words
come out.

I ask God please
to guide my hand
with anything I have to do.
so what I make
is beautiful
and maybe useful,
too.

God's the only One who knows
the thoughts we're thinking
in our minds.
I read good books
    and think good thoughts
        so He'll be pleased
            with what He finds.

I ask God's blessing
on my feet
whenever I go
out to play.

He'll keep me happy,
safe, and sound,
and out of trouble
all the way.

It's better to say
"thank you"
than always to say
"please".
I thank Him
for all sorts of things
— like spider webs,
and bees.

I thank Him for His woodsy world,
where you can hear things
you can't see.
The squirrels, hiding,
scold at you,
and birds call out
from every tree.

I thank God
for all living things
— the ones that
live for just
a day,

~the ones who live
a long, long time,
so slow
and wrinkled up
and gray.

I thank God 'specially
for time.
There's such a lot
to see and do
and hear,
I have to ask God please
to show me how
to use each year.

At night before I go to bed,
I get down on my knees to pray
(which is the best way,
if you can).
I thank Him
for a lovely day.

And just before
I go to bed,
and just when I've
turned out the light,
I know He's somewhere
very near.
I smile at Him
and say "Good night!"

Innovations
in the Design of
Electrical
Transmission
Structures

Proceedings of a Conference sponsored by the Structural Division of the
American Society of Civil Engineers

in cooperation with the
Institute of Electrical and Electronics Engineers
Electric Power Research Institute
University of Missouri at Kansas City

Kansas City, Missouri
August 14-16, 1985

Edited by Gene M. Wilhoite

ASCE
1852
®

Published by the
American Society of Civil Engineers
345 East 47th Street
New York, New York 10017-2398

Copyright © 1986 by the American Society of Civil Engineers,
All Rights Reserved.
Library of Congress Catalog Card No.: 85-73731
ISBN: 0-87262-511-7
Manufactured in the United States of America.